CHRISTMAS MAGIC
25 WILD HOLIDAY ADVENTURES

SHORT STORIES FOR KIDS 8-12

Table of Contents

Introduction

Welcome to a world of winter wonder and Christmas magic!

In these pages in front of you, there are twenty-five adorable adventurous tales that will warm your heart and spark your imagination. Follow along with courageous reindeer, magical snowmen, curious children and a peek into Santas world as they uncover the true spirit of the season. From daring escapes to heartwarming friendships, each story is a special gift, filled with adventure, joy, and the extraordinary magic that makes this time of year so special.

So, get cozy, turn the page, and read one story and the book will last all Christmas long or let yourself get lost all at once in twenty-five magical and independent adventures.

The Great Reindeer Race

Pip was the fastest reindeer at the North Pole. He could zip through the snowy fields and dodge snowdrifts faster than any of the others. His hooves were a blur, his mind a whirlwind of speed. But there was one problem: he was terrified of flying. The annual Great Reindeer Race, which determined who would lead Santa's sleigh, was his dream, but the thought of leaving the ground made his hooves feel like jelly. Pip knew he needed to get over his fear of flying to realize his dream, he just didn't know how.

His best friend, Holly, a graceful flyer with a kind heart, noticed how scared Pip was every time he tried to fly. "You're the absolute fastest on the ground, Pip," she said, her voice gentle. "You just need to trust your wings."

Every afternoon, Holly took him to the tallest mountains at the edge of the North Pole. The first time, Pip could barely look down without his legs trembling. Holly would show him how to catch the wind, how to dip and soar with ease. When Pip was going to try, Holly encouraged him. "Just a little jump, Pip. I'm right here," she said. He started with tiny hops, then a short glide down a small slope. The fear was still there, a knot in his stomach, but with Holly by his side, the knot began to loosen. Soon, he was taking longer flights, always with Holly flying beside him, her encouraging smile a constant light in the sky.

When the starting bell for the race rang, Pip shot off like a rocket. The other reindeer leaped into the sky, their antlers catching the crisp air. Pip stayed low, following the familiar path, but soon a swirling, magical cloud of glittering snow blocked his way. The only way through was up. The old fear crept back, a cold shiver down his spine. But then he remembered Holly's words, her patient lessons on the mountaintops.

He closed his eyes, took a deep breath, and launched himself into the air, the memory of Holly's steady gaze gave him confidence and pushed him forward. At first he got so surprised that his stomach flipped, but then a strange feeling of lightness took over. He wasn't just flying; he was dancing with the wind. He found a pocket of clear air inside the cloud and zipped through, emerging on the other side just as the other reindeer were struggling.

Pip glided across the finish line, a feeling of pure joy in his heart. He had overcome his fear and he had won! This was his big dream to win the race. But the greatest prize wasn't the spot leading Santa's sleigh, it was the thrill of having wings. That Christmas Eve, as he led the team into the starlit sky, Pip wasn't afraid. He was home, and he knew he couldn't have done it without a friend who believed in him.

The Sleigh's Annual Tune-Up

The air at the North Pole buzzed with a festive energy. With just three days until Christmas Eve, the final preparations were in full swing. In the grand Sleigh Bay, two apprentice mechanics, Buddy and Luna, were putting the finishing touches on Santa's sleigh. Their master, the wise old elf Barnaby, had entrusted them with the most important task: the final check.

"It has to be perfect," Buddy said, running a gloved hand over the sleigh's gleaming red surface. "This is for the Christmas flight the one flight everything has to work."

Luna nodded, her eyes twinkling with a shared secret. "Which is why we're giving it our own little upgrade." Hidden beneath a workbench was their masterpiece: a small, crystalline sphere they called the **Aura-Amplifier**. It was designed to magnify the magic of the sleigh, making Santa's journey more joyful.

They pulled out their detailed schematics of the sleigh's core, unrolling it across the workbench. "The power conduit runs under the seat," Luna pointed out, her finger tracing a line. "We need to tap in there, but it's a tight fit."

Buddy used a miniature, glowing chisel to gently open a panel. "If we place it here, it'll get a direct connection to the magical engine." He paused, looking at the crystalline sphere. "But what about the vibration? It could knock the amplifier out of balance."

"You're right," Luna said, a thoughtful frown on her face. She rummaged through her toolkit and pulled out a small, feathered mallet. "We'll use this to tap it into the navigation core instead. It's more stable there, and we can link it directly to the Christmas spirit sensors." They worked with a quiet, practiced rhythm, Buddy holding the amplifier steady while Luna used a tiny, enchanted soldering iron to secure the magical connections. The crystalline sphere hummed to life with a soft, warm glow, but a small light on the dashboard began to flicker.

Buddy leaned in, his brow furrowed. "The power flow is a little uneven."

Luna immediately knew what to do. "We need to recalibrate a little!" With a few precise adjustments and a gentle tap of her mallet, the flickering stopped, and the sphere's glow became steady and bright. The two apprentices shared a high-five, their faces alight with a mix of relief and pride.

With a shared look, Buddy and Luna hopped into the sleigh. They didn't have any reindeer, so they used a magical wind-up key. As Buddy turned it, the sleigh lifted off the ground, gliding smoothly out of the bay and into the swirling snow. They pressed the button for the **Aura-Amplifier**.

Immediately, the sleigh's path changed. It didn't just glide; it danced. It spun in gentle spirals, leaving a trail of shimmering stardust that swirled with the snowflakes. The sleigh bells didn't just jingle; they chimed with a perfect, harmonious melody that echoed across the winter landscape. The test flight was a beautiful, serene ballet through the sky, and Buddy and Luna watched in awe as their little gadget turned the sleigh into a masterpiece of Christmas magic.

When they landed, Barnaby was waiting for them, a broad smile on his face. "I felt that all the way from my workshop," he said, patting them both on the shoulder. "A fine job, indeed. This Christmas Eve, the children won't just hear the sleigh; they'll feel its music in their hearts." Buddy and Luna knew they had just done more than a tune-up; they had added a new layer of magic to Christmas.

The Lost Present

The Johnson family was a bit like a tornado in a candy shop, a flurry of good intentions and delightful chaos. On Christmas Eve, they scurried off a bustling city bus, their arms overflowing with shopping bags, cheerful chatter filling the snowy air. But in their rush, a small, wrapped gift, a special, hand-whittled toy boat for their youngest, Leo, slipped unnoticed from under a coat and tumbled quietly to the floor.

As the bus pulled away, a pair of shimmering tinsel garlands clinging to the bus windows, Sparkle and Glitter, noticed the forgotten parcel. "Oh, dear!" Sparkle whispered, her silver threads trembling. "That poor little present is all alone!"

Glitter, a bright red strand with tiny bells, jangled with determination. "We can't just leave it here. We have to help it get home!"

They quickly enlisted the help of an adventurous Gingerbread Man air freshener hanging near the driver's seat. His name was Spice, and he was known for his love of puzzles. "A lost present?" Spice exclaimed, his cinnamon-scented arms waving. "This is a mission! The bus will be turning around soon. We can't wait for the return trip, we have to get it to them now!"

Together, they hatched a daring plan. As the bus slowed at the next stop, Spice, with the help of a wind chime snowman, carefully rolled the present towards the open door. Just as it seemed they would make it, the doors began to close.

But a brave Nutcracker ornament, perched on a seat back, lunged forward and propped the door open with his stiff, painted hands. The gift rolled out onto the curb, where it landed in a soft pile of snow.

A streetlamp blinked on, and a chorus of street-corner carols filled the air. The present, with its bright red bow, began to glow. As the city watched, a gentle breeze lifted the gift, floating it through the air like a paper lantern. The Nutcracker waved goodbye as the gift soared over rooftops and twinkling streetlights, guided by the music and the silent wishes of the holiday decorations.

The toy boat landed gently on the Johnsons' front porch, a silent messenger of Christmas magic. Leo rushed to the door, his eyes wide with wonder at the

sight. "My boat!" he gasped, his heart swelling with joy. And as the family gathered around the found present, the decorations on the city bus smiled, knowing their small act of kindness had brought a bit of Christmas magic to life.

The Christmas Mailroom

Elara was the quietest elf in Santa's North Pole mailroom. While others loudly sorted letters into towering stacks, she worked in the silent, dusty corners, carefully cataloging letters that had been sent to the wrong address. On Christmas Eve, the main hall buzzed with last-minute deliveries, but Elara's corner was already quiet. The last packages had been sent, and the last letters sorted. Or so she thought.

As she was about to close her ledger, a tiny, crumpled envelope caught her eye. It had slipped behind a conveyer belt and was smudged with soot. Elara gently picked it up, her heart aching. It was from a boy named Timmy, and the handwriting was shaky. He didn't ask for a toy. He simply wished for his mom, a soldier far away, to be home for Christmas. Elara looked at the clock. It was nearly midnight.

Santa's sleigh would be lifting off any minute.

Her quiet nature usually kept her from a bold act like this, but she couldn't leave this letter here. This wish was too important. Without a second thought, she tucked the letter into her apron and raced out of the mailroom.

She dodged hurried elves with baskets of wrapping paper and jumped onto a conveyer belt for oversized presents, using it like a high-speed shortcut to the workshop. She vaulted over a stack of video games and slid down a slide meant for teddy bears, landing in a pile of soft, fluffy stuffing. The loud, cheerful workshop seemed impossibly far away, but she pushed on, her small feet a blur.

As she burst through the doors to the launchpad, the sight took her breath away. Santa's sleigh, magnificent and enormous, was already loaded. The reindeer were stomping their hooves, their noses glowing bright. Santa, with a twinkle in his eye, was about to climb into the driver's seat.

"Santa, wait!" Elara shouted, her voice small but surprisingly strong. He turned, and a friendly, surprised smile spread across his face. Elara, out of breath and holding the letter tight, ran to him. She quietly explained about Timmy who wrote the letter and about his story. Santa listened intently, his expression softening.

"A very important delivery," he said, taking the crumpled envelope. He placed it in a special pocket on his red coat, right over his heart. "Thank you, little one. This is the most important gift of all."

As the sleigh disappeared into the starry sky, Elara watched from the ground. Her heart swelled with a feeling she had never known, not just warmth, but a quiet, powerful joy. She had been the one to deliver the most precious wish of all.

The First Ski Trip

Lily felt as if she were a character in a movie. The snow-covered mountains rose majestically around her, and she pictured herself gracefully carving lines into the pristine powder. Her new ski suit felt amazing, and her brand-new skis were polished to a gleam. This was it, her first family ski trip, and Lily was sure she would be a natural.

Her confidence lasted until the bunny slope. The moment she strapped into her skis, she felt clumsy and unbalanced. The instructor, a cheerful man named Ben, tried to show her how to form a wedge with her skis and glide with them parallel, but Lily's legs seemed to have a mind of their own. She wobbled forward, arms flailing, and tumbled into a soft, powdery snowbank. Her skis tangled, and she struggled to untangle them while Ben patiently laughed and offered a helping hand.

The rest of the morning was a blur of tumbles. She slid backward, fell sideways, and at one point, managed to faceplant just as a group of toddlers zipped past her. Hot tears of frustration pricked her eyes. This wasn't graceful. This was humiliating. As she sat in the snow, a knot of tangled skis and hurt pride, she wanted to scream, "I quit!"

Just as she was about to unbuckle her boots, Ben skied over and knelt beside her. "Hey, it's okay," he said softly. "The snow is soft, and it's a great day for making snow angels, isn't it?" He helped her up and looked her in the eye. "Every single person on this mountain fell down their first time. And the second time. And probably the third. Don't worry about being perfect. Just focus on one thing. Can you slide forward and stop by bringing the tips of your skis together?"

Lily's parents watched from the lodge, giving her a thumbs-up. Her dad mouthed, "You've got this." With their encouragement and Ben's simple advice, Lily took a deep breath. She didn't try to go fast or look like a pro. She just focused on making her feet form a wedge shape. She slid a few feet, felt her skis spread, and stopped. It wasn't perfect, but she didn't fall. A genuine smile, the first of the day, spread across her face.

The next morning, the gleam was gone from Lily's skis, replaced by scuffs and scratches. Her enthusiasm was gone, too, replaced by a sense of dread. "Do I have to go today?" she asked her mom at breakfast, poking around in her scrambled eggs.

"You don't have to do anything you don't want to," her mom said gently, "but I'm going to guess you'll feel a lot better once you get back out there."

Lily sighed, but as they walked to the slope, she remembered Ben's words: "Every single person fell down their first time." Today wouldn't be about being perfect. It would be about learning. She put on her skis, and instead of feeling clumsy, she felt a little more grounded. She remembered the feeling of her feet forming the wedge shape.

On the bunny slope, she took it slow. Instead of a messy tumble, her first fall was a controlled, slow-motion slide. She laughed instead of crying. When Ben saw her, he just gave her a small, encouraging nod. This time, she focused on doing one thing at a time: first, a wobbly wedge to control her speed, then a tentative turn while trying to keep her skis parallel. The whoosh of the wind in her ears as she slid forward was exhilarating.

By the end of the morning, she was making her way down the slope in a series of careful, controlled turns. It wasn't fast, and it wasn't graceful, but it was skiing. When she finally reached the bottom, her parents were there, cheering. "That was incredible, sweetie!" her dad exclaimed. Her heart swelled with pride. It was still pretty hard, and she had a long way to go, but now she was finally on the right path.

The Secret of the Snowglobe

The attic door always sounded like a grumpy old giant clearing its throat. Ten-year-old Ellie pushed it open just wide enough for her and her younger brother, Tom, to slip through.

"Are you sure they hide them up here?" Tom whispered, his eyes huge in the dusty shadows. He was seven, and the mission—finding their parents' secret stash of Christmas presents—felt like an operation straight out of a spy movie.

Ellie clicked on the heavy flashlight. A dusty yellow beam cut through the air, making the swirling dust motes look like tiny, frantic fairies. "Dad always says, 'If we can't find it, it must be in the attic,'" she quoted with the authority of the older sibling. "And we definitely haven't found them anywhere else."

Ellie started with a stack of labeled cardboard boxes near the chimney. "Taxes,

2018." Nope. "Old Blankets." Definitely not. "Baby Clothes (Tom)." No.

Tom, meanwhile, was less systematic. He kicked at an old chair in the corner. "Nothing here," he mumbled, about to give up. Then Tom saw an old snow globe that caught his attention.

The old snowglobe sat on a high shelf in the attic, forgotten and dusty. Inside the snowglobe it looked like a small, sad world. Unlike other snowglobes, this one had no swirling glitter. Its tiny gingerbread houses were dark, and the little figures of snowmen and elves stood still, looking glum.

"Look Ellie, I bet it's broken," Tom sighed, reaching for it. As his fingers touched the glass, a faint warmth spread through the globe. The glass shimmered, and the dusty scene inside began to glow. A magical pull, like the feeling of falling into a soft cloud, enveloped the siblings. When their feet touched solid ground, they were no longer in the attic.

They stood in the middle of a gingerbread village, just as it had appeared in the globe. The air smelled of cinnamon and warm sugar. But the village was silent. There was no Christmas music, no cheerful chatter, no laughter. The gingerbread town square, though decorated with candy cane arches, felt empty. Even the lights on the peppermint lampposts barely flickered.

A little gingerbread boy with a cracked smile approached them. "Welcome," he said, his voice quiet. "We are so glad you are here. Our Christmas spirit has gone missing." He explained that a cold wind had blown through the village one night, taking with it all the joy of the holiday. The village's spirit was tied to their love of Christmas, and without it, they were just sad gingerbread folk.

Ellie and Tom knew what they had to do. They told the villagers their favorite Christmas memories of decorating the tree, singing carols with their family, and the delicious smell of their mom's Christmas cookies. As they spoke, a small, golden light began to emanate from their hearts, filling the quiet square. The light danced and swirled, bringing color back to the decorations and a twinkle to the elves' eyes. The little gingerbread boy's smile mended itself.

The village's spirit, once lost, was found. A wave of joyful energy pulsed through the village, and a soft glow surrounded Ellie and Tom. They found themselves back in their attic, holding the snowglobe. This time, the gingerbread village was bright and alive, with tiny gingerbread villagers dancing and singing. They hadn't found what they were looking for when they first went up to the attic, but they had found something much better. The siblings knew they had helped the village find its Christmas spirit, and with it, they had found their own and it didn't matter anymore were the Christmas presents were hidden.

Preparing the Suit

In the grand sewing room of the North Pole, where spools of glowing thread spun like galaxies, lived two of Santa's most dedicated seamstress elves, Noel and Cookie. Their final, most important task of the year was the last-minute inspection of Santa's famous suit. On the afternoon of Christmas Eve, with the smell of gingerbread and pine in the air, they carefully lifted the heavy red velvet from its silk hanger.

"It's magnificent," Noel whispered, running a hand over the fabric. "Not a single crease."

But as Cookie carefully smoothed a sleeve, she saw it: a tiny, shimmering thread near the cuff, hanging loose like a single, silver snowflake. It was the enchanted thread that held the suit's magic. Without it, the suit's warmth and durability would fade.

"Oh, no," she gasped. "It's the thread of the North Star!"

They both knew this wasn't an ordinary stitch. Their finest needles were too dull, their sturdiest thread too weak. This was a magical thread, and it needed a magical fix. They huddled together, their small faces filled with worry. "We have to use a celestial stitch," Noel said, remembering a lesson from their apprentice days. "But how do we create one?"

With no time to lose, they rushed to the oldest, dustiest corner of the sewing room, where the Great Book of North Pole Seamstresses rested. They frantically flipped through the pages until they found the entry they needed: "To mend the thread of the North Star, one must use the Needle of Starlight, found only in the Star-Weaver's Box."

They found the box tucked away, and inside, a single, glowing needle awaited them. It shimmered like frozen light. Working together, they took the celestial needle and, with steady hands and focused minds, began to weave. It wasn't like sewing; it was more like painting with light. The threads on the suit seemed to dance, pulling themselves toward the needle and weaving themselves back into the velvet. The loose thread snapped back into place, sealing the tiny gap as if it had never been there. The repaired section of the suit now glowed with a faint, beautiful light.

As they finished, Santa arrived, his jolly laugh echoing through the room. "Thank you, my little weavers!" he boomed, pulling the suit on. He ran a hand over the repaired spot, and a look of pure delight crossed his face. He knew their stitch had made his suit even stronger, powered by their·dedication and courage. Noel and Cookie watched him fly into the night, their hearts full of the secret knowledge that their tiny, invisible stitch was helping to make Christmas perfect for all.

The Tree That Wished to Be Lit

In the back corner of Mr. Peterson's Christmas tree lot stood the scrawniest, most forgotten pine tree. While its grander neighbors were wrapped in string and carried away on car roofs, this little tree remained. It was thin, crooked, and its needles were a bit sparse. But in its heart, it held a powerful wish: to be chosen. It dreamed of being decorated with glittering ornaments, wrapped in tinsel, and, most of all, of having its own string of lights that would make it shine like a star.

As the lot grew emptier, a woman named Clara walked in, shivering and looking utterly exhausted. She didn't look at the trees with the usual holiday joy; her face was drawn, and her eyes were tired. Christmas wasn't an exciting time for Clara anymore; it was just a blur of deadlines and endless tasks. She needed a tree for a small apartment, something simple. She sighed, her gaze sweeping over the remaining trees.

Suddenly, the little pine felt a warm, hopeful flicker inside. It wasn't a spark, but a gentle, golden glow that seemed to come from within its very core. The light was so faint that no one else could see it, but Clara, whose heart felt so cold, was inexplicably drawn to it. She walked past all the perfect, symmetrical trees and stopped right in front of the little forgotten pine.

"Hello there," she whispered, her fingers tracing a rough branch. The tree's glow intensified, and a faint, sweet scent of pine filled the air, like a forgotten memory. As she stood there, Clara felt something she hadn't felt in years: a hint of peace. She saw the little tree not for its crooked branches but for its quiet beauty and the tiny, magical light that seemed to be for her alone.

Clara smiled for the first time that week. "You're the one," she said, her voice filled with a warmth she hadn't known she had.

She took the little tree home, and when she hung a single string of lights upon it, its inner glow combined with the twinkling bulbs, illuminating her entire room. The tree had its wish, and in doing so, it had helped an unlikely person rediscover the true spirit of Christmas.

The Day the Snow Stole the Gray

The rain had been a constant companion for two weeks. Ten-year-old Oscar sat at the window, his forehead pressed against the cold glass, watching the world outside dissolve into a monotonous, misty gray. It wasn't just a light shower; it was a cold, steady, bone-chilling downpour that seemed determined to wash away every last bit of Christmas spirit. The Christmas tree lights that had once seemed so magical now cast a feeble glow against the gloom. The festive carols on the radio sounded tired and flat, and even his mom's famous gingerbread cookies smelled less of holiday cheer and more of a damp, forgotten pantry. With only three days left until Christmas, Oscar felt a heavy, sinking feeling in his stomach. He was sure Santa's sleigh would need a boat this year.

As Tuesday afternoon wore on, the rain began to slow, turning into a few lazy drips from the gutters. The air grew still, so quiet that Oscar could hear the gentle sound of a single snowflake hitting the windowpane. He straightened up, his heart giving a tiny, hopeful thump. Another snowflake landed, then another. Within minutes, the gray world outside was being painted over with a pure, brilliant white. Oscar let out a whoop and raced to the closet, pulling on his warmest coat, hat, and gloves. He didn't even bother to zip up before flinging open the back door.

Milo, his golden retriever, was a blur of happy motion. The moment his paws touched the fresh powder, he launched himself into a series of joyful spins, his tail wagging so hard his entire body wiggled. Oscar laughed, grabbing Milo's favorite red ball and launching it into the pristine blanket of white. Milo dove headfirst into the snow, emerging a moment later with a fluffy white mustache and the ball firmly in his mouth, shaking his head with a playful growl. They spent what felt like hours playing fetch, running and tumbling in the fresh, clean snow. They took a break to lie side-by-side, creating two very different kinds of snow angels: Oscar's a perfect outline of a boy with outstretched arms, and Milo's a blurry, happy impression of a dog.

Finally, with the sun beginning to cast long, orange shadows across the backyard, Oscar grabbed his sled. He and Milo raced to the big hill behind his house. He hopped on, and Milo, sensing the fun, gave the sled a playful nudge, sending them both flying down the slope with happy shouts echoing through the quiet, cold air. As they reached the bottom, Oscar lay in the snow, breathless and giddy. He looked at Milo, whose ears were now coated in white, and felt a rush of unbridled joy. The magic he'd been looking for wasn't in the Christmas lights or carols, but in the simple, beautiful moment of playing in the snow with his best friend.

Mrs. Claus's Secret Workshop

In a cozy corner of the North Pole, just off the main hallway leading to Santa's office, was a tiny workshop that smelled of cinnamon, sugar, and something else, something warm and magical. This was Mrs. Claus's secret workshop, a place where she didn't just bake treats, but where she mended broken dreams.

One chilly afternoon, Santa entered, his face not quite as jolly as usual. "My dear, I found this letter tucked behind a chimney," he sighed, handing her a crumpled, tear-stained envelope. "It's from a little boy named Finn. He didn't ask for a new toy, but for his grandfather's old toy train, which broke and was thrown away. His wish is impossible."

Mrs. Claus took the letter and read it. Her smile, which could warm a whole room, softened. "Nothing is impossible, dear," she said. She walked to a cabinet filled with jars of shimmering, iridescent powders. For a wish like this, she needed a special ingredient: the **Tears of Forgotten Wishes**, a crystalline dust gathered from the silent moments after a wish has been given up on.

She carefully measured her ingredients: flour as white as new snow, sugar that sparkled like frost, and a pinch of starlight. But the most important step was stirring in the magical dust. As she stirred, she hummed a gentle tune, infusing each cookie with warmth and hope. She shaped them into tiny toy trains, each one as unique as a snowflake.

As the scent of magic filled the workshop, she carefully placed a single train cookie on a small, velvet pillow. That night, Santa added the pillow to his sleigh. He didn't know how the magic would work, only that it would.

The next morning, Finn woke up feeling a familiar ache of sadness. He went to his backyard to play, the snow had started to fall but Finn couldn't really find the joy.

Suddenly, he saw something peeking out from under a bush. It was his grandfather's toy train, not broken but perfectly whole, as if it had simply been misplaced. He picked it up, his heart swelling with a joy so pure it felt like sunlight.

Back at the North Pole, Mrs. Claus smiled, knowing her secret ingredient had done its work. The cookie had brought more than just sweetness; it had brought back a lost memory and mended a little boy's dream.

The Feast of the Yule Lads

In Iceland, children are lucky enough to be visited by not one, but **13 pranksters** called the **Yule Lads** in the 13 nights leading up to Christmas! These friendly-but-naughty troll-like brothers come down from their home in the mountains, one by one, to visit towns and farms. **Stekkjarstaur** (say it like: Steck-yar-stower), whose name means **"Sheep-Cote Clod,"** is the **very first Yule Lad** to arrive, usually on the night of December 11th.

Stekkjarstaur is the eldest of the Yule Lads, who are the sons of the scary troll, Grýla, and her husband, Leppalúði. Like his 12 brothers, Stekkjarstaur leaves a little surprise for Icelandic children. Every night, children place one of their **shoes** on the windowsill. If they have been good that day, Stekkjarstaur leaves a **small gift** like a sweet treat, a tiny toy, or a piece of candy in the shoe. But if a child has been naughty, they might wake up to find a **rotten potato** instead! Stekkjarstaur starts the fun and his brothers are coming the following nights.

The chill of the Icelandic winter had settled over the little village, but inside Anna's home, the air was warm with the scent of freshly baked gingerbread cookies. It was the night before the first of the thirteen Yule Lads was set to arrive, and Anna's mother had a serious look on her face. "Remember, Anna," she said, her voice a low whisper, "tonight is for Stekkjarstaur. You must leave your best shoe on the windowsill. If he finds a clean, polished shoe, he might leave a sweet surprise. But if it is dirty..." she trailed off, leaving the threat of tricks unsaid. Anna's heart fluttered with a mix of excitement and unease. The thought of being pranked by one of the mischievous lads made her scurry to polish her favorite red shoe until it shone like a ruby.

That night, Anna tucked her shoe onto the windowsill, the glass pane cold against her little hand. She lay in her bed, her ears straining for the sound of clattering hooves. It was said that Stekkjarstaur, or "Stilty-Goat," had wooden legs and loved to pester sheep. Anna imagined his tall, awkward form tapping along the icy path outside her window. The house was silent, save for the wind howling a lonely tune. A few minutes later, Anna heard a faint creak from outside. She pulled the wool blanket up to her chin, her eyes wide with a combination of fear and anticipation. Had he come? She held her breath, praying her shoe was shiny enough.

The sun rose slowly, painting the sky in strokes of pink and gold. Anna, having barely slept, leaped from her bed and raced to the window. The shoe was still there, right where she had left it. She peeked inside, her smile growing with each passing second. Resting on the bottom was not a lump of coal, but a beautifully carved wooden puffin, its little beak painted bright orange and its wings a smooth, pearly white. Anna gently picked it up, a wave of relief and pure happiness washing over her. She hugged the little puffin close, her face radiating with a big, joyous grin.

She knew she had done everything right. She had followed the tradition, respected the lads, and in return, had received a gift more precious than any candy. As she looked out at the snowy landscape, she felt a sense of magic swirling in the air. Twelve more nights remained, twelve more shoes to polish, and twelve more chances for a trick or a treat. But with her carved puffin clutched in her hand, she felt ready for whatever came next.

The Whispering Christmas Lights

Lucy and Noah's house was covered in more lights than all their neighbors' combined. Their dad, a man who loved Christmas with a blinding passion, had a knack for decorating. But this year, a new string of old, glowing bulbs had a secret. As the siblings sat on their porch, gazing at the sparkling display, a soft, faint sound reached them, like tinsel rustling in a gentle breeze.

"Do you hear that?" Lucy whispered.

Noah leaned closer. "Sounds like... a whisper?"

They pressed their ears against the house's siding, trying to find the source. The whispers grew clearer. "Under the fir... a friend is stirring..."

The kids exchanged a look. There was a small, potted fir tree on the porch. Beneath it, they found a tiny, dusty treasure map rolled up and tied with a ribbon. It was the first clue.

The lights seemed to hum with excitement as they followed the next clue, their whispers leading them to the garage. "By the workshop's door, a snowy friend waits for more." The workshop was where their dad kept his tools, and propped against the door was a snowman ornament with a faint glow. He held a small note that said, "Check the frosty pane, where stars softly rain."

They ran inside, their excitement building. They found a frosty windowpane, and when they breathed on it, a faint image appeared, a drawing of the mantelpiece.

The lights on the house outside blinked rhythmically, a silent cheer.

On the mantel, nestled behind a stack of cards, was a small, ornate key. The whispers now came from every light, a chorus of tiny voices. "The music box waits... for a friend of all fates." The music box, a gift from their grandma, usually sat closed on a shelf. But when they used the key, it opened with a gentle click. Inside wasn't a ballerina or a tune, but a small, silver bell tied with a red ribbon.

The front door opened, and their parents came in, smiling. "We thought you might enjoy a little scavenger hunt," Dad said.

Lucy and Noah looked at the magical bell in their hands, then back at the lights outside, which winked in a joyous, multi-colored sparkle. The real treasure, they realized, wasn't the bell but the wonderful, magical feeling of the hunt itself. From that day on, the lights always seemed to hum a little tune just for them, a constant reminder of the day their house's Christmas decorations helped them find the true spirit of the season.

The Great Gingerbread Escape

Gary the Gingerbread Man woke up with a start. The oven door had just opened, and a monstrous, shadowy hand reached in, lifting his friend Gus off the baking sheet. It was then that Gary realized his purpose in life wasn't to be a decoration, it was to be a snack! He looked around at the other cookies, their faces still decorated with sleepy, frosting smiles. He had to act fast.

"We must escape!" Gary whispered, his voice a crunchy little sound. "Before it's too late!"

He rallied his troops: two gingerbread girls named Ginny and Gabby, and a whole army of tiny gingerbread friends. Their first challenge was the long, perilous countertop. A river of spilled milk stood between them and the safe, dark corner of the kitchen. With a brilliant flash of inspiration, Gary grabbed a candy cane from a nearby bowl and used it as a bridge. One by one, the gingerbread friends scurried across, their little legs a blur of motion.

Next, they faced the towering mountain of dirty dishes. Gary, nimble and brave, led the way, climbing up a teacup handle and sliding down a fork to a plate below. They moved like a well-oiled machine, their mission clear: save themselves and find a new home.

But their biggest obstacle was the cat, a fluffy creature named Mittens who was always on the prowl for crumbs. Mittens' ears twitched, and his eyes narrowed as he spotted them.

"Run!" Gary yelled, and the gingerbread army scattered.

Just as Mittens pounced, Gary threw a jelly bean, hitting a glass on the counter. The loud clink startled the cat, giving them just enough time to disappear into the darkness under the kitchen cabinets. They found a tiny opening near the floor, a space big enough for them to squeeze through. It led to a dark, hidden world filled with old toys and dust bunnies, a place no human would ever find them.

The gingerbread family had found their new home. They spent the rest of the night sharing stories of their great escape, their hearts pounding with the thrill of victory and the promise of a long, happy life far from the cookie jar. They were no longer just gingerbread cookies; they were adventurers, and their tale of bravery would be whispered for Christmases to come.

HOPE YOU LIKE IT SO FAR

I'd Love to Hear From You!
Please Continue Reading!

When you finish reading a review
would mean so much to me ❤

If you found the book helpful,
inspiring, or just enjoyable, would
you take a moment to leave a
review? Your feedback not only
helps others but also keeps me
motivated to create more valuable
content for you.

Your kind words make a big difference.
Thank you for your support!

The Toymaker's Apprentice

Levi, a young apprentice with a heart full of dreams, worked in Master George's dusty toy shop. The shop was filled with wooden soldiers and painted dolls, but it lacked a certain magic. Master George was a master craftsman, but his face was perpetually set in a frown, and he grumbled more than he spoke. He would simply say, "Toys are for playing, not for wishing."

One night, after closing, Levi saw a flicker of light from the back of the shop. He saw Master George push aside a wall of old crates, revealing a hidden door. Curiosity won over caution, and Levi tiptoed behind his master.

Inside was not a workshop, but a whirlwind of light and color. The air hummed with a soft, pulsing energy, and half-finished toys floated in the air, waiting for their finishing touches. In the center, a swirling vortex of shimmering starlight pulsed, illuminating the entire room.

"What is this place?" Levi whispered, his eyes wide with wonder.

Master George turned, his grumpy facade crumbling into weary resignation. "It's the heart of Christmas," he sighed. "A workshop powered by Christmas wishes." He gestured to a pile of glowing letters.

"Each one is a child's wish, sent straight here. But there are too many, and my heart has grown too old to keep up."

Levi saw the sadness in his master's eyes. "But... they're beautiful," he said, touching a toy soldier that glowed faintly. "You just need help. I want to make toys that sparkle with magic, too."

Master George looked at Levi, seeing the genuine spark in his eyes. A small, almost imperceptible smile touched his lips. "Perhaps," he said, his voice softer than Levi had ever heard it. "Perhaps you're right."

He handed Levi a half-finished train, its wheels still dull. Levi's hands, filled with newfound purpose, began to work. As he carved the last detail, he thought of a child's joyous squeal. The train began to glow brightly, a brilliant beacon of Christmas magic. Levi smiled, and for the first time, Master George smiled back. The secret workshop had found its new heart, and two very different toymakers had found a shared joy.

Lucia's Light

Saint Lucia Day, or Lucia (say: Loo-see-ah), is one of the most beautiful and heartwarming traditions in Sweden, celebrated every year on December 13th, right when the winter darkness is at its deepest. This festival is all about bringing light, warmth, and hope into the long Scandinavian winter, pointing the way to Christmas.

The tradition is led by a girl chosen to be Lucia, who is dressed in a flowing white gown with a red ribbon tied around her waist. Her most famous feature is the crown she wears on her head: a wreath of green lingonberry or evergreen branches with real or battery-powered candles that shine like a bright halo. Lucia is followed by a procession of other girls who also wear white gowns and often carry a single candle, boys wearing white gowns and cone-shaped hats decorated with stars. Younger children sometimes join the line dressed as adorable gingerbread people or elves.

The Lucia procession moves slowly and serenely through the darkness in homes, schools, churches, and hospitals while singing the beautiful, traditional Lucia song and many other Christmas songs.

The story behind this beloved day has two parts. One part is about an ancient belief in Sweden that the night of December 13th was the longest and most dangerous night of the year, filled with evil spirits, which is why people needed to stay up late and eat many big meals. The other, more famous part, comes from a Christian saint named Lucia, who lived long ago in Italy. Legend says that she was a kind girl who secretly brought food to Christians hiding in dark tunnels, and she wore a wreath of candles on her head so her hands were free to carry as much help as possible. The Swedish Lucia tradition blends these two stories together, making it a wonderful festival that brings light and kindness to everyone during the darkest time of the year.

Ingrid was a girl of quiet corners and whispered words. She loved the tradition of Saint Lucia's Day more than anything, a festival of light that always seemed to cut through the long, Swedish winter darkness. But the thought of being the town's chosen Ingrid, leading the procession with a crown of candles, filled her with a familiar dread. The crown felt too heavy, the song too loud, and the many eyes from the town seemed too bright.

When Ingrid was chosen as the town's Lucia and it was announced at the town square Ingrid's heart pounded like a drum. She wanted to hide, to disappear into the crowd. But her grandmother squeezed her hand and whispered, "Your light is the softest, my dear. And those are often the most needed."

On the morning of the procession, Ingrid's hands trembled as her mother helped place the crown of lingonberry leaves and electric candles on her head. Her white gown flowed around her, and her voice, usually so small, felt trapped inside her chest. But as she began to sing the traditional song, something shifted. Her voice, though soft, was clear, and the light from her crown cast a gentle, warm glow in the pre-dawn darkness. The children behind her, each holding a single candle, followed her lead. She wasn't just a girl anymore; she was the bearer of light.

The procession made its way through the sleepy streets, a moving constellation of warmth. As they approached the last house on the lane, Ingrid's heart skipped a beat. It belonged to old Mr. Olsson, a man known for his perpetual frown and a garden gate that was always bolted shut. The talk of the town was that his grumpiness came from a deep, old loneliness. He had lost his wife many years ago and the holidays only seemed to make his sadness worse.

Ingrid hesitated, but then remembered her grandmother's words. She held her head high and, with her little band of children, approached his front door. She sang the hymn "Sankta Lucia" in a voice as gentle as falling snow.

Inside, Mr. Olsson heard the faint melody. He shuffled to the window and saw the glowing crown. The sight, the sound, the simple, pure joy of it all, reached into a place in his heart he thought had been cold forever. He saw not just a procession, but a memory of his wife on a similar morning long ago. A single tear traced a path down his cheek. He unbolted his door, a sound not heard in years, and looked at Ingrid. "Thank you, sweet kids," he said, his voice cracking. "You've reminded me of what matters."

Ingrid smiled, and it was a new kind of smile, confident and bright. Her light had found its way through the darkness, not by being loud, but by being true.

The Unwanted Holiday Sweater

The air in the living room thrummed with excitement. Torn wrapping paper lay like a colorful sea around Charlie's feet, but his focus was on the last present; a large, perfectly wrapped box from his Aunt Carol. Unlike his parents, who bought him practical things, Aunt Carol always sent something unique and special. This year, he was sure it was the new video game console he had been wishing for. He carefully peeled back the festive paper, his heart pounding with anticipation. But as he lifted the lid, his smile faded. Inside wasn't a sleek gaming box, but a lumpy, knitted thing. His shoulders slumped. He pulled it out, a monstrous, green-and-red-striped with a glittery reindeer whose nose lit up when a button was pushed. It was the ugliest sweater he had ever seen.

"It's so... festive," his mom said, trying to hide a laugh.

Reluctantly, Charlie put it on. The moment the wool touched his skin, a strange warmth spread through him. The room felt brighter, and the Christmas carols on the radio sounded more joyful. When he pushed the reindeer's nose, it not only lit up but began to hum a soft tune that made the gingerbread cookies in the kitchen rise and dance. A sudden urge to dance himself overwhelmed him, and he found his feet tapping a rhythmic beat. His family cheered, delighted by the magical performance.

That night, Charlie wore the sweater to bed. When he woke up, he felt lighter, as if he could float. He looked in the mirror and realized he was hovering an inch off the ground. The reindeer's nose pulsed with a gentle light, and the humming from earlier filled the air. With a thought, he floated higher, bumping into the ceiling. The sweater had magic! It was no longer ugly, but a key to an incredible new world.

Over the next few days, Charlie discovered more of the sweater's powers. By twisting one of the bells on a sleeve, he could make his cookies fly. By pulling a loose thread, he could create a sparkling trail of snowflakes behind him. He didn't care what his friends would think anymore; this sweater was a secret, a source of endless fun and magic.

On Christmas morning, he wore the sweater with pride. It wasn't just a garment; it was a magical artifact. As he raced down the stairs, he didn't have to run, he simply glided, a boy on a cloud of Christmas cheer, wearing the most wonderful, magical, and ugly sweater in the world.

The Snowman Who Hated the Cold

Frizz was not like other snowmen. While his friends, with their rosy carrot noses and twiggy arms, reveled in the frosty air, Frizz shivered. He hated the cold. He longed for sunshine, for the feel of warm earth beneath his packed snow feet, and for the soft rustle of leaves instead of the harsh whistle of the wind. He was built for winter, but his heart belonged to summer. He would spend his days dreaming of golden fields and lazy afternoons, wondering if there was a place a snowman could be warm and not melt away.

One blustery afternoon, he overheard two squirrels chattering about an old legend. "They say the 'Summer-Winter Tree' can grant the wish of warmth to any creature of the cold," one whispered. "It's said to grow on the sunniest side of Whispering Mountain."

A spark of hope lit up inside Frizz's coal eyes. This was his chance! With a quiet determination, he bid his friends farewell and began his great adventure.

His journey was not easy. The wind tried to steal his scarf, and he had to slide down a steep, icy hill, but the thought of warmth kept his spirit high.

He met a family of arctic foxes who pointed him toward the mountain. He even had a chat with a grumpy badger who told him a shortcut through a frozen stream.

Finally, after what felt like an eternity, he saw it. Atop a small hill, bathed in a shimmering, golden light, stood a majestic tree. One half was covered in frosted, silver leaves, glistening with ice. The other half was ablaze with golden, leafy branches, swaying gently as if in a summer breeze. A magical aura of warmth radiated from the golden side, so cozy and inviting. Frizz, with a feeling of pure joy he had never known, made his way to the tree and stood under the golden canopy.

He felt the warmth seep into his icy body, but to his surprise, he didn't melt. The magic of the tree was keeping him perfectly formed, a snowman in his own personal summer. He had found it, a home where he could be a snowman and be warm. Frizz no longer hated the cold; he had simply found his place in the sun.

The Train to the North Pole

Jack and his younger sister, Maya, had one rule for Christmas Eve: no peeking. But how could they resist? Tucked under the twinkling lights of the Christmas tree was the most incredible toy train set they had ever seen. It was a miniature masterpiece, with a tiny red engine and cars so detailed they could almost see the tiny passengers inside.

"I wish it were real," Maya whispered, her nose pressed against the window. "I wish it could take us to the North Pole."

As if in answer, a soft, golden light pulsed from the train's chimney. The miniature wheels began to turn, and a low rumble echoed through the room. Jack gasped as the train grew, its metallic red body expanding, its steam stack puffing white clouds into the air. In moments, the toy was a life-sized locomotive, its engine glistening in the glow of the Christmas tree lights.

"Climb aboard!" a cheerful voice chugged from the engine.

They scrambled into the first car, and with a hiss of steam, the train burst through the front door, leaving a trail of glitter and magic in its wake. They weren't on tracks anymore, but gliding through the air over the sleeping neighborhood. Below, streetlights looked like scattered jewels and houses were soft, glowing squares in the dark.

The train soared higher, past the moon, which seemed close enough to touch. They watched as the northern lights painted the sky with swirling ribbons of green and blue. The world felt quiet and vast, and they were the only ones awake to see its magic. They passed a forest of pine trees, each one dusted with snow and shimmering with an inner light.

Finally, the train descended into a valley bathed in a warm, golden glow. Below them, a city of ice and light shimmered. They could see Santa's grand workshop, a flurry of activity even in the late hour, and the reindeer stables where their antlers seemed to catch the starlight. The train slowed to a stop, its cheerful voice bidding them farewell. "You've made it! Now for your real adventure."

As the train turned around and chugged back, a feeling of peaceful joy settled over Jack and Maya. When it came to a stop in their living room, it was back to its tiny, miniature size. But now, when they looked at it, they knew a secret no one else did: the true magic of Christmas lay not in the toys themselves, but in the belief that they could come to life.

The Portal in the Fireplace

Dylan was a boy who loved Christmas more than anything, but he always felt a little sad when it was over. One blustery December afternoon, as he helped his dad tidy up the living room, he noticed something strange about the fireplace. The flames didn't flicker; they danced in perfect, swirling spirals, and the heat didn't feel like fire. It felt like a warm, comforting hug.

"What's wrong, sport?" his dad asked, but Dylan didn't hear him. The swirling flames parted, revealing a shimmering, green-and-red tunnel. Curiosity overpowering his fear, Dylan took a deep breath and stepped through.

He tumbled out onto a soft, snowy street lined with candy cane lamp posts. It was snowing, but the flakes were made of gingerbread, and the air smelled of peppermint and pine. Ahead, houses were decked out with lights that hummed with a quiet, joyful energy. He realized with a gasp that it was Christmas morning. He saw a clock on the town hall steeple and knew that here, it would always be Christmas.

Dylan played with magical toys, ate endless gingerbread, and even rode a carousel made of rocking horses. He did everything he had ever dreamed of doing on Christmas Day.

But as the "day" went on, he started to miss the special feeling of Christmas at home, the one day of the year that made it so magical. He walked back to the fireplace portal, which was now a glowing opening in the town square.

He stepped back into his living room, just as his dad turned to him, looking puzzled. "You've been standing there for a while, are you okay?"

Dylan smiled, a real, genuine smile. "I've never been better," he said. He had a new secret, and he now understood that Christmas wasn't just about endless celebrations, but about the joy of having that one special day. He couldn't wait for tomorrow, because every day leading up to Christmas was its own kind of magic.

The Friendship From a Snowman

In a quiet house on a quiet street, lived a boy named Liam who often felt a little lonely. His best friends were the books on his shelf and the characters in his imagination. When the first big snow of the winter fell, Liam put on his winter clothes and went outside. He spent all afternoon building the most magnificent snowman he had ever created. He gave him a carrot nose and arranged a few small pebbles into a gentle smile. He called his creation Frosty.

As dusk settled, a strange, beautiful light shimmered around Frosty. The snowman's pebble eyes blinked open, and his smile widened. "Hello, Liam," a voice as soft as falling snow whispered. Frosty wasn't a normal snowman; he was a magical creature from the North Pole, sent to find a friend in need of a little Christmas magic.

Liam wasn't scared. He was filled with a joy he hadn't felt in a long time. For the next two days, they were inseparable. Frosty taught Liam how to slide down the steepest hills without a sled, gliding on the icy air as if they were flying. They built snow castles and decorated them with icicles that chimed like tiny bells. Frosty's laughter was a crisp, joyful sound that echoed through the quiet neighborhood.

But as Christmas Eve drew near, the air grew warmer. Frosty's buttons began to droop, and his nose turned to slush. "I must go back to the North Pole now," he explained softly. "The magic of Christmas is calling me home."

Liam's heart sank, but he understood. Frosty gently took Liam's hand and placed a single, glowing snowflake into it. "Keep this," Frosty said. "It's filled with our magic. When you feel lonely, just hold it, and remember that even though I'm far away, our friendship is a forever kind of thing."

With a final wave, Frosty melted into a swirl of shimmering snow and vanished. Liam stood there, alone again, but the little snowflake in his palm glowed with a warm, steady light. He wasn't lonely anymore. He was the boy who had a secret friend from the North Pole, and that was a kind of magic that would last all year long.

The Christmas Star Catcher

Jenny lived in the quiet, snow-dusted village of Everglow, where the magic of Christmas was said to be woven into the very fabric of the sky. Each year, the great Christmas Star would hang above the village, its light ensuring the spirit of the season never waned. This year, however, something was wrong. On Christmas Eve, the star began to shimmer and tremble, its brilliant light flickering like a candle in a draft. The town elders gathered, their faces etched with worry. "The star is falling," the oldest among them announced, his voice barely a whisper. "It is losing its magic. Only a heart full of hope and a spirit of true bravery can catch it before it fades forever."

Jenny, who was no older than ten, listened from the edge of the crowd. While the adults spoke of a seemingly impossible task, a warm determination filled her. She knew she had to try. She grabbed her father's sturdy net, normally used for catching fireflies in the summer, and a small lantern to light her way. She wasn't the strongest or the fastest, but her heart was filled with a deep, unwavering love for Christmas.

She climbed the tallest mountain behind her village, the frosty wind biting at her cheeks and the snow crunching under her boots. Each step was a struggle, but she kept her eyes on the trembling star, now much closer than before. It pulsed with a weak, fading light, casting long shadows across the icy landscape. The air grew colder, and a sense of dread began to creep in. But just as she felt a shiver of doubt, she thought of the joy on her family's faces, the warmth of the carolers' songs, and the scent of gingerbread wafting from her home.

Reaching the summit, she could see the star clearly, a tiny, fragile point of light slowly drifting down. It was no longer the brilliant beacon it once was, but a faint whisper of its former self. Holding her breath, Jenny stretched out the net, her arms trembling with effort. As the star floated past, she swung the net with all her might, catching the tiny, glowing orb just before it hit the ground. The moment it touched the net, it burst with a dazzling light, and a wave of warmth spread through her. The Christmas Star was safe. Its light was brighter than ever, and a cheer of relief echoed up from the village below. Jenny smiled, knowing she had done the impossible.

The Secret Code of the Candy Canes

The air in Grandma Evelyn's cozy home hummed with the quiet magic of Christmas Eve. Ten-year-old Owen and his older cousin Mia sat by the crackling fire, a mountain of gift wrap and discarded ribbons at their feet. They had torn through the presents and were now in that peculiar post-holiday lull.

"I'm bored," Owen announced, stretching.

Grandma Evelyn, seated in her armchair, chuckled. "Well, you've still got my candy canes to get through." She gestured to a large, clear jar on the mantelpiece, filled with her famous, hand-pulled candy canes. Unlike the store-bought ones, these were slightly lumpy and irregularly twisted, each one a unique shade of red and white.

Mia picked one out, the peppermint scent filling the air. As she unpeeled the plastic, she noticed something odd. "Hey, these have little marks on them. Look, Owen."

Owen grabbed a cane and squinted. Tiny, deliberate-looking dots and dashes were etched into the white swirls. They weren't random imperfections; they were a pattern.

The cousins began to unwrap the candy canes one by one, laying them out on the rug. They noticed the pattern changed subtly on each one. One had two dots, the next a dot and a dash, and the one after that had three dashes. As they continued, a realization dawned on Mia.

"It's a code," she whispered. "Grandma always said her gingerbread recipe was a family secret. What if this is how she hid it?"

Working together, they lined up all the candy canes they had unwrapped. It wasn't Morse code, as they first suspected, but something simpler. When a pattern of dots and dashes repeated, they realized it represented a letter, just like a simple substitution cipher. The first few canes spelled out "LOOK IN..."

Excitement surged through them. They continued unwrapping, their methodical work revealing a longer message: "LOOK IN THE OLD COOKBOOK ON THE TOP SHELF."

They scrambled to the kitchen, their eyes darting to the towering bookcase of recipes. On the very top shelf, tucked behind a few worn-out baking tins, was a small, leather-bound book with no title. Inside, written on the very first page in their grandmother's elegant cursive, was the legendary family gingerbread recipe, passed down from her own mother.

Grandma Evelyn came into the kitchen, a knowing smile on her face. "Found it, did you? That's how my mother and I used to share our favorite recipes. A little game for Christmas."

Owen and Mia grinned, holding the book like a treasure map. They had not only found the secret to a delicious holiday treat but also uncovered a wonderful new family tradition.

The Great Sled-Building Competition

Oliver and his best friend, Maya, stared gloomily at their old, flimsy plastic sleds. "They're just not fast enough," Oliver declared, kicking a mound of snow. It was a week before Christmas and the neighborhood sledding race was coming up, and they knew they needed something better than what they had. A mischievous grin spread across Maya's face. "Why buy a new one when we can build a better one?" she suggested.

Their mission led them to the treasure trove of Oliver's garage. It was a wonderland of old furniture, discarded tools, and half-finished projects. They found a long, sturdy piece of wood that used to be a shelf, perfect for the base. For runners, they found an old, scratched pair of skis. "They're not exactly sled runners," Oliver mused, "but they'll be slick enough." The biggest find was a dusty bicycle handlebar, which they decided would be their steering wheel.

Building their masterpiece, which they named "The Garage Rocket," was an exercise in patience and problem-solving. First, they had to saw the skis to the right length, a task that required both of them to hold steady. The handlebars wobbled no matter how tightly they screwed them in, threatening to come loose on the first big turn. "We need more support," Maya said, her brow furrowed. They found an old clothesline and wove a tight web of rope around the handlebars, tying them securely to the base. The seat, a salvaged milk crate, proved even more troublesome, sliding off with every bump. After several tries, they finally secured it with a handful of bent nails and some strong, waterproof glue. They worked for days, their fingers numb from the cold, but their excitement kept them going.

Finally, the day of the race arrived. The neighborhood kids had sleek, shiny new sleds, but Oliver and Maya's creation was a one-of-a-kind. It was clunky and a little crooked, but it was theirs. They took their position at the top of the hill. Oliver sat in the front, gripping the handlebar, and Maya braced herself behind him. "Ready?" she shouted.

"Ready!" he yelled back. They pushed off, and "The Garage Rocket" flew. It wasn't the fastest sled, but it turned and carved with a grace none of the others had. They didn't win first place, but as they crossed the finish line to cheers from their families, they knew they had won something even better: the pride of having built their own adventure.

The Magical Toy Factory

It was Christmas Eve, and ten-year-old Wesley's father had a surprise for him. "Come on, sport," he said with a wink. "I have to make a quick delivery to the old toy factory downtown, and you can come with me."

Wesley had always found the factory a bit gloomy. Its brick walls were gray, and the windows were grimy with age. He expected to see tired workers packing boxes, but when he stepped inside, the air was filled with a strange, sweet scent of pine and gingerbread. A cozy fire crackled in a huge fireplace, and soft, tinkling music floated from somewhere deep inside.

His father headed to the office, leaving Wesley to explore. He wandered past massive conveyor belts and looming machines, all silent and still. A small, wooden door with a brass bell caught his eye. He pushed it open and peered into a brightly lit workshop.

Wesley gasped. The room was not empty. Tiny figures, no taller than his hand, were buzzing with energy. They wore miniature green coats and pointed red hats. They were elves! With nimble fingers, they were stitching the ears onto a teddy bear, painting rosy cheeks on a doll, and winding up a tin soldier. They worked with a joyful concentration, humming along to the music.

A little elf, no bigger than a teacup, noticed him. "Don't just stand there, lad!" He shouted. "We have a deadline, you know!" He pointed to a pile of unfinished wooden trains.

Wesley, mesmerized, spent the next hour helping the tiny elves. He couldn't quite believe it was real. When his father came to get him, the workshop was silent and empty once more. The door was gone. All that was left was a perfectly carved wooden train, sitting on the dusty floor, with the initials "L.N." etched into its base. Wesley knew then that he would have the best Christmas ever, because he had been a part of the real magic of it all.

Santa's Summer Vacation

This years Christmas had come to an end, the last present was delivered, and every single reindeer was tucked in and dreaming of carrots. For Santa Claus, the big man with the even bigger laugh, it was time for the moment he looked forward to almost as much as Christmas Eve itself: vacation!

"Phew!" Santa sighed, leaning back in his big red armchair. "A job well done, Mrs. Claus, wouldn't you agree?"

Mrs. Claus, busy knitting a tiny scarf for one of the elfs, smiled warmly. "The best, dear. Now, where will it be this year? Far, far away from the snow, I hope."

Santa's eyes twinkled. "Oh, I've got just the place! It's an unlisted location, known only to a few friendly sea turtles and a particularly chatty parrot. I call it' ...The Hidden Cove of Perpetual Sunshine'!"

With a swift, almost silent movement that belied his size, Santa slipped out of his heavy red coat, exchanging it for a vibrant, flower-patterned Hawaiian shirt and a pair of very comfortable blue shorts. Instead of his sleigh, he packed a small, enchanted suitcase that held everything he needed (mostly sunscreen and a very thick novel) and whistled for his ride.

Out of the frosty air swooped a magnificent, emerald-green macaw named Mango. Mango wasn't a reindeer, but he was certainly the fastest flyer south of the North Pole. Mango took Santa on his back and they flew south.

Their journey was a blur of clouds, stars, and salty air. Finally, Mango dipped low over the shimmering, cerulean ocean. Below them was an island so lush it looked like a giant, green velvet cushion. Tucked into the far side of the island was the Hidden Cove.

It was absolute paradise. The sand was almost as white as snow, the water was so clear you could count the colorful shells at the bottom, and the air smelled wonderfully of coconut and blooming jasmine.

"Ah, bliss," Santa murmured, hopping down onto the warm sand.

He immediately kicked off his black boots. Oh, the relief! His toes, usually encased in warm fur and leather, wiggled happily in the sand. He sat down in the sand and settled in.

For a full week, Santa did nothing but rest. He was a man of simple pleasures, and this quiet beach was all he needed.

He didn't make toys; he built magnificent, but utterly useless, sandcastles. He didn't check lists; he snorkeled with friendly schools of iridescent fish, marveling at the coral reefs. He didn't deliver gifts; he delivered funny jokes to Mango, who would squawk with laughter and repeat them to the waves.

One sunny afternoon, Santa was floating peacefully on a giant inflatable candy cane. His big, hearty laugh was quiet now, a gentle, happy rumble as he drifted. A little sea turtle, its shell decorated with swirling patterns, poked its head out of the water.

"Excuse me, sir," the turtle squeaked politely, "Are you... are you that famous toy-maker?"

Santa smiled, tipping his sun hat. "That depends. Am I on your nice list?"

The turtle giggled. "Oh, absolutely! My cousin got a wonderful little submarine last year. But you look so different! Where is the red suit? And the snow?"

"The snow is on pause, little friend," Santa explained, splashing water gently. "Even Santas need to recharge their magic batteries. This sunshine and quiet is what gets me ready for next Christmas. I'm filling up on happy energy!"

The sea turtle looked at the peaceful, rested Santa, his face glowing with a healthy tan instead of rosy from the cold. The big man looked truly relaxed.

"Well," the turtle said, dipping his head respectfully, "I'm glad you have your sunshine. Please have a wonderful rest, Mr. Claus."

As the sun set on the final day, painting the sky in shades of pink and orange, Santa knew he was ready to head home.

He gave Mango a fond scratch, waved goodbye to the sea turtles, and took one last, deep breath of tropical air.

"Home, Mango!" Santa boomed, his voice full of its usual cheer. "Time to get to work! We've got a world of wonderful toys to make!"

And with a joyful whoosh, Santa Claus flew back towards the snowy North Pole, his heart full of sunshine and ready for another year of giving.

THANK YOU!
FOR CHOOSING THIS BOOK!

I'd Love to Hear From You!

A review would mean so much to me ❤

If you found the book helpful, inspiring, or just enjoyable, would you take a moment to leave a review? Your feedback not only helps others but also keeps me motivated to create more valuable content for you.

Here's how you can leave a review:

1. Scan the QR code on this page to go directly to the review page
2. Or, visit your Amazon Orders page, find this book, and click "Write a Product Review"

Your kind words make a big difference. Thank you for your support!

Made in the USA
Monee, IL
31 October 2025

33285743R00085